Fabulous

Barkcloth

Dedication

To my mother, Priscilla Smith, who instilled in me
a love for sewing and all textiles at a very early age.

Fabulous Barkcloth

Home Decorating Textiles from the 30s, 40s & 50s

Loretta Smith Fehling

Schiffer Publishing Ltd

4880 Lower Valley Road, Atglen, PA 19310 USA

Designed by Bonnie M. Hensley
Type set in UnivrstyRoman Bd/Zurich BT

ISBN: 0-7643-0837-8
Printed in China

Published by Schiffer Publishing Ltd.
4880 Lower Valley Road
Atglen, PA 19310
Phone: (610) 593-1777; Fax: (610) 593-2002
E-mail: Schifferbk@aol.com
Please visit our web site catalog at **www.schifferbooks.com**

In Europe, Schiffer books are distributed by Bushwood Books
6 Marksbury Avenue Kew Gardens
Surrey TW9 4JF England
Phone: 44 (0)181 392-8585; Fax: 44 (0)181 392-9876
E-mail: Bushwd@aol.com

This book may be purchased from the publisher.
Include $3.95 for shipping. Please try your bookstore first.
We are interested in hearing from authors with book ideas on related subjects.
You may write for a free printed catalog.

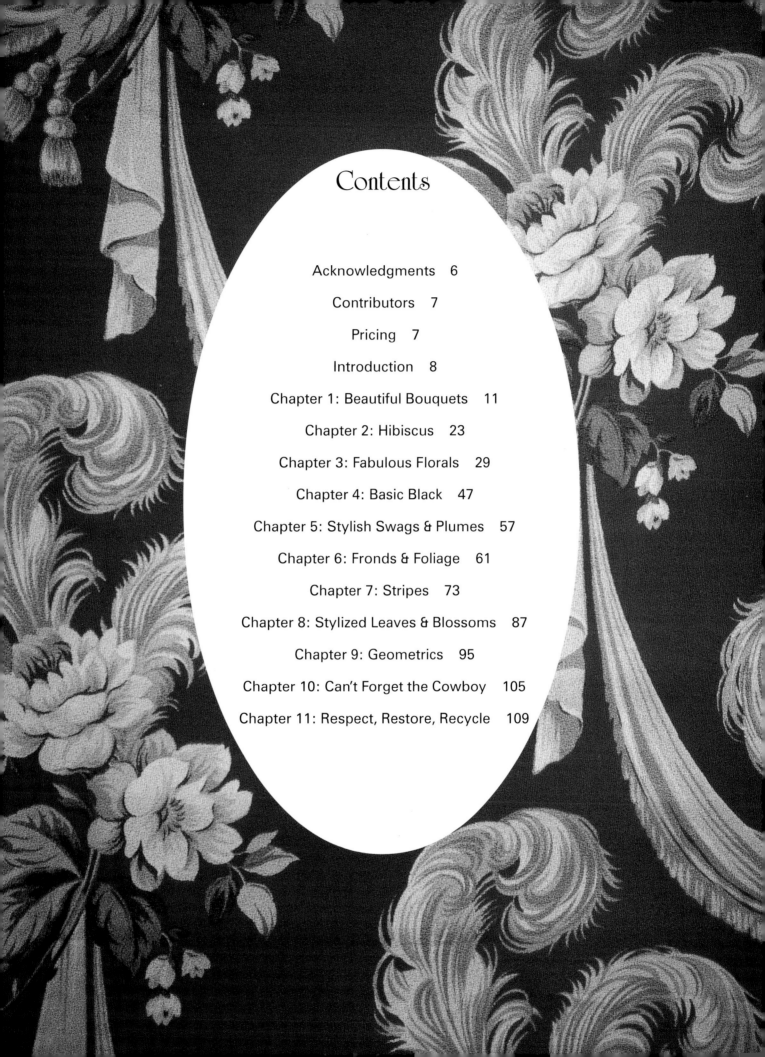

Contents

Acknowledgments

A special thanks to Margaret Meier for searching out vintage fabrics and allowing many of them to be photographed for this book.

Contributors

Margaret Meier, owner
Vintage Fabrics
3500-C. N.E. 11th Ave.
Fort Lauderdale, Florida 33334
(954) 564-4392

Turtle Creek Antiques
850 W. Armitage
Chicago, Illinois 60614

Pricing

*I*t's impossible to put average prices on barkcloth. Price swings for a single drapery panel are very wide. Prices vary depending on what part of the country you're shopping in, as well as the quantity of fabric and the condition it is in. We all must decide what we want to pay for a small part in our rich textile history.

Introduction

The intention of this volume is to document pictorially many of the outstanding textiles used in our homes from the 1930s to the present. Barkcloth, named such for its reference to tree bark, is the primary focus. Today, the word barkcloth generically refers to many of the home decorating textiles of our past. Actually, barkcloth is a type of cotton weave that is very dense as well as textured.

In the past, barkcloth was most often used for draperies or to make slipcovers that were often changed with the seasons. I can remember when my mom made her first set of matching draperies and slipcovers. The drapes were completely lined and the slipcovers fit perfectly. She was very proud of her work and the matching drapes and couch meant a great deal to her. She had privacy, a beautiful floral print to cheer up the house, and I know that she felt she had arrived at a new level of social acceptability.

These fabrics were moderately priced and the average homemaker could afford to cover her windows with beautiful drapes. I recently purchased some yardage that was originally sold at a department store in Indianapolis. It still had its original price tag of 69 cents a yard! I think of what these fabrics cost today and imagine what a fine time our mom's and grandma's must have had when they went fabric shopping.

In recent years, barkcloth has enjoyed a renaissance. Many people have begun collecting these wonderful fabrics and using them in today's homes. Barkcloth draperies are again adorning windows or being reworked to cover couches and chairs. I found twelve drapery panels that matched and had a slipcover made for my couch. It always brings a smile to my face when I walk in the door! Smaller pieces of barkcloth are being used to make purses and pillows. I use original barkcloth to cover lampshades and to construct vests and jackets. I've seen others use barkcloth to cover photo albums, hat boxes, and vintage luggage. Modern designers are using vintage barkcloth as inspiration for today's textiles.

Familiar feeling designs are showing up on windows, couches, and on clothing.

Magnificent floral designs always seem to be a favored subject matter for barkcloth. Bouquets of peonies, roses, poppies, carnations, and daisies are frequently used. We also see calla lilies, lilac, gladiola, ginger, and my favorite, pussy willow. When I started collecting and using barkcloth for my line of clothing, it seemed I saw pussy willow everywhere I turned. It inspired me to plant some in my yard.

This book includes an outstanding orchid print and many different hibiscus. The hibiscus is included in many of the tropical motifs, which make me think of Miami Beach circa 1946. Tropical paradises were created using many types of fronds, bamboo, and beautiful blossoms. Chapter Six, Fronds & Foliage, includes what I consider one of the most typical and recognizable designs of the era. The design examples are shown in white, yellow, seafoam green, and blue colorways. I've also seen this design on burgundy and black backgrounds.

Hollywood inspired many of our more elegant patterns. Large sweeping designs of flowers held together with swags of fabric and accented with plumes can be found. These designs were often very large in scale, but found their way to windows that were covered ceiling to floor and wall to wall. Recently, I watched the movie *The Birdcage* on television and noticed one of these wonderful designs hanging on windows in the film.

Basic black background barkcloth seems to be the most sought after by collectors and the most difficult to find today. Collectors love the strong contrast of colors against the black background. I've included over twenty black background examples that show mostly floral designs printed in gorgeous colors. The most glorious example of orchids that I've seen is in the first photograph of Chapter Four, Basic Black.

Stripes played a big part in barkcloth design. The stripes are often designs of intertwining fronds or flowers on one color that are separated by solid areas of a second or multiple colors. These designs were meant to coordinate with some of the all-over floral designs, just like you might see with stripes or plaids today. Barkcloth often came in widths of 36 inches, and I have found drapery panels sewn together by alternating a floral with its coordinating stripe. Seamstresses needed to make draperies wide enough to fit their picture windows and sometimes they use this creative method to fill their needs.

As barkcloth design progressed in the 1950s, the yardage took on a more stylized appearance. Specific flowers were harder to identify in the designs, and geometric shapes were often mixed with organic shapes and swirls. It sometimes appears that the designs have taken inspiration from block printing. This geometric/organic theme then progressed to strictly geometric and occasional representational designs. The fabric designers seemed to be inspired by scientific abstraction. Were they influenced by the onset of the space program? I wonder what types of prints the first group of astronauts had hanging in their family rooms?

The 1950s was also the era for Roy Rogers, The Lone Ranger, and all the other television and Saturday matinee cowboys. No book would be complete without thinking of them and the romantic western themes. Barkcloth examples include highlights of western life in the designs. I'm sure many boy's rooms and family rooms were adorned with these western themes.

Often the selvage edge of the fabric adds to the story. Here, company names were printed, and sometimes the title of a particular design appeared. Included in this volume are fabrics from companies with this printing on the selvage edge:

A Confab Co. Vat Print
A Coronet Guaranteed Vat Print
A Covington Vat Print
Goldco Vat Print
A Joana Fabric Design
Markwood Fabrics
A Puritan Print
Saison Happily Married Fabrics
A Spectrum Original Vat Color Print
A Standish Fabric
Tilbury Fabrics
Waverly Bonded Fabric

As a full-time designer making one-of-a-kind garments from vintage barkcloth and other vintage textiles, "Respect, Restore, Recycle" is the mantra for my textile search. Finding enough barkcloth in good condition for me to make a jacket is becoming more difficult each day. I search antique malls and shops wherever I travel and also visit large antique shows in hopes of finding draperies or unused yardage for my garments.

Chapter 1
Beautiful Bouquets

Opposite page: A Puritan Print

Joana Fabric "Pussywillow"

A Waverly Bonded Fabric "Stratford"

15

Markwood Fabrics

21

Chapter 2
Hibiscus

A Goldco Print "Judson"

Tilbury Fabrics "Buckingham"

Chapter 3
Fabulous Florals

A Spectrum Original

A Goldco Vat Print

A Standish Fabric

A Joana Fabric Design "Bermuda"

Chapter 4
Basic Black

A Spectrum Original Vat
Color Print

Saison Happily Married Fabric

A Covington Vat Print

50

A Spectrum Print

"Cascade"

Chapter 5

Stylish Swags & Plumes

Chapter 6
Fronds & Foliage

A Confab Co Vat Print

Tilbury Fabrics "Fantasy"

A Spectrum Original

63

A Rite Fit Fabric

70

Chapter 7
Stripes

Opposite page: Saison Happily Married

Spectrum Original Vat Color Print

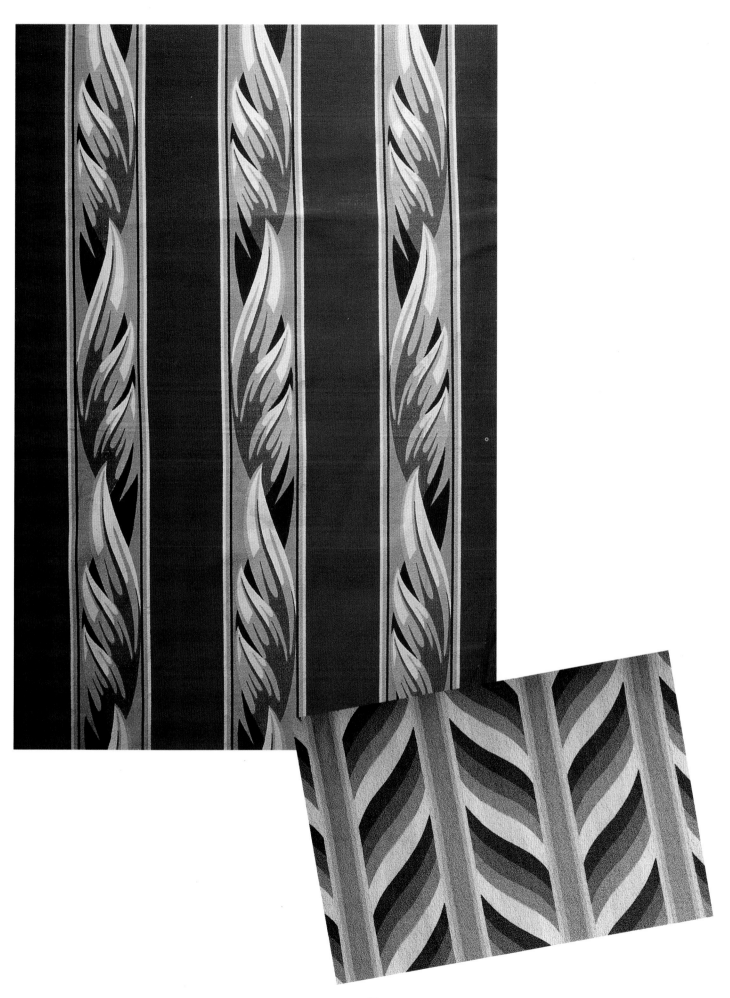

Chapter 8
Stylized Leaves & Blossoms

A Goldco Vat Print "Comstock"

Opposite page: Saison Happily Married Fabric

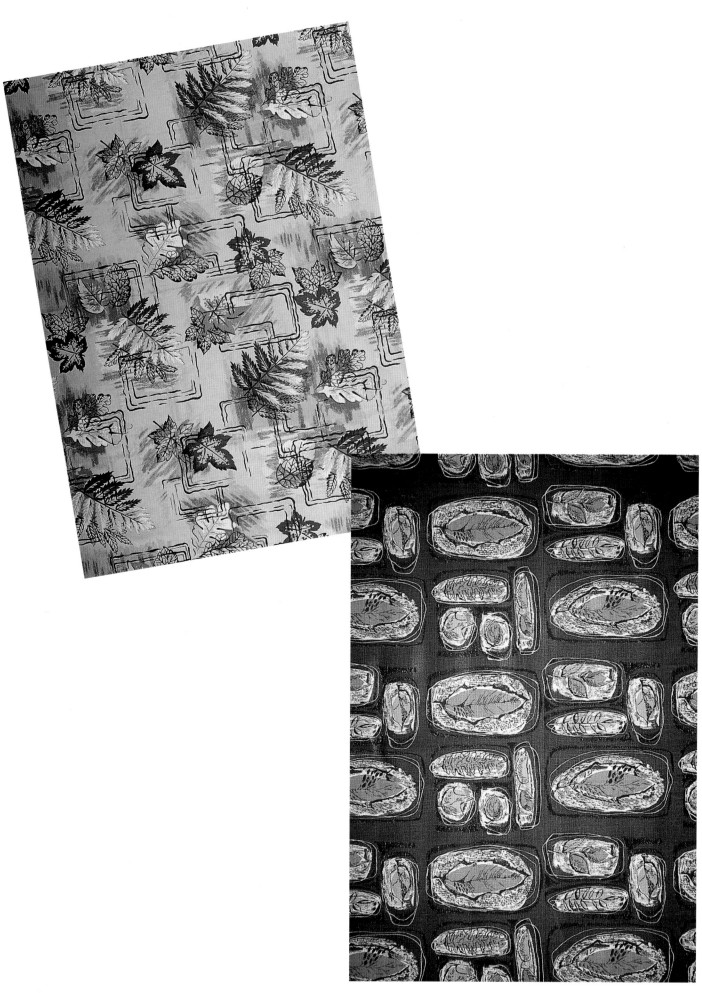

A Spectrum Original

Saison Happily Married Fabric

A Spectrum Original

A Coronet Guaranteed Vat Print

96

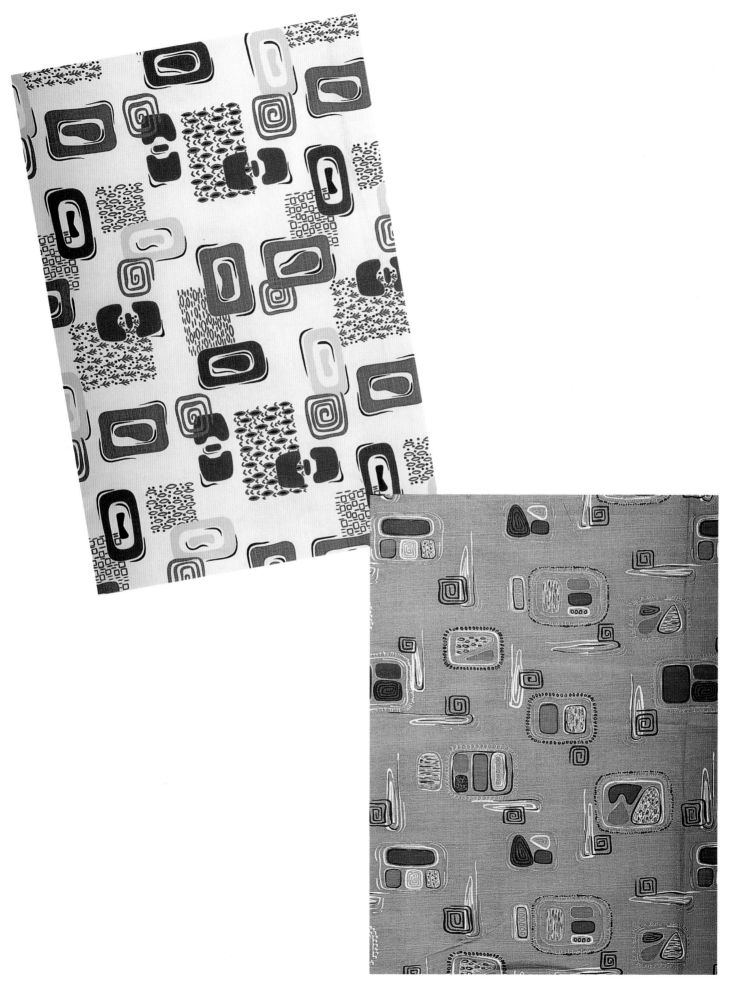

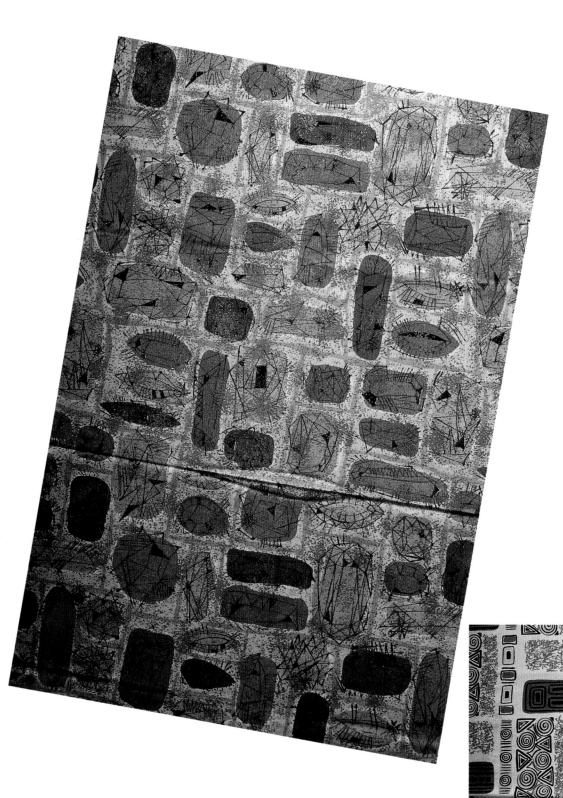

Chapter 10
Can't Forget the Cowboy

Saison Happily Married

Chapter 11
Respect, Restore, Recycle

The following photos are *courtesy of Hunt's Studio in Portland, IN.*

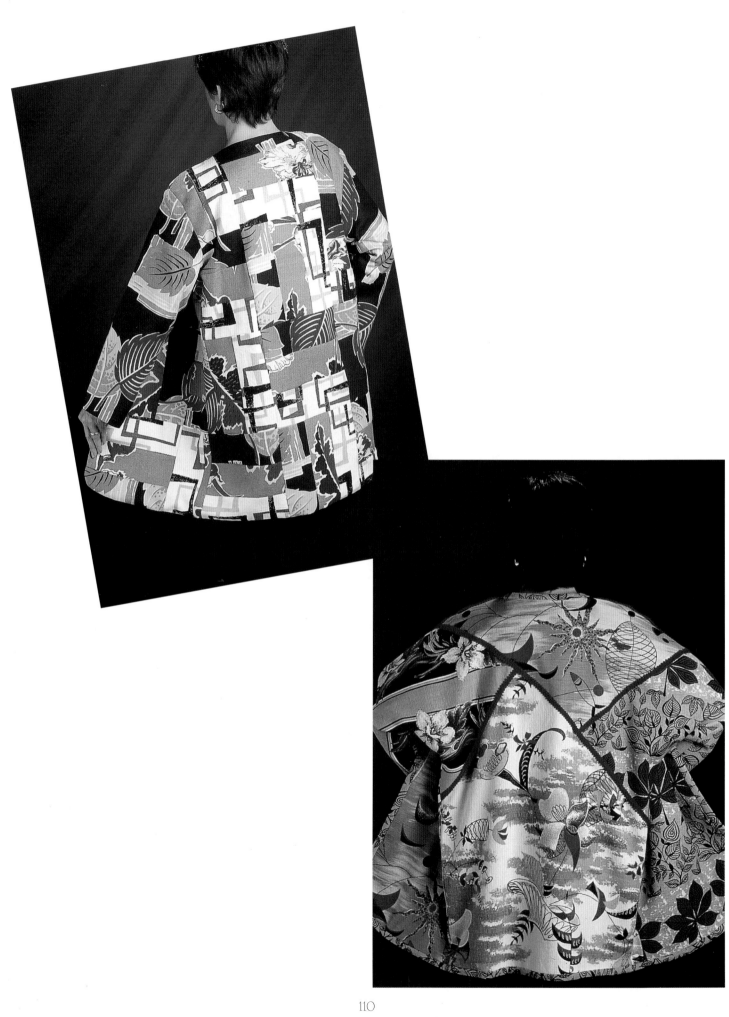